THE COAST

A full appreciation of the nature and implications of physical geography can only be achieved through an understanding of the immense natural forces which strive unceasingly to alter the face of the land. In this completely new and absorbing series of introductory books for junior school children, Margaret Lloyd Davies has set out, in a clear and precise style, step by step explanations of the processes involved in the evolution of the most common coastal features.

As well as various model-making activities which can be confidently undertaken by children either alone or in groups, the book contains numerous attractive and clear line illustrations and thus provides a most comprehensive introduction to this particular aspect of physical geography. Further titles in the series include *Lowlands* and *Mountains and Hills.*

THE AUTHOR

A qualified teacher, Margaret Lloyd Davies spent eight years as the Head of the Geography Department at a girls' grammar school. She has travelled extensively abroad and lives with her husband and son in Kent.

THE COAST

Margaret Lloyd Davies

Illustrated by

Angela Lewer

FREDERICK MULLER LIMITED

First published in Great Britain 1977
by Frederick Muller Ltd,
London NW2 6LE

ISBN 0 584 63544 3

Printed and bound in Great Britain by
REDWOOD BURN LIMITED
Trowbridge & Esher

We are all very lucky in that we live on a relatively small island. Not many places are more than one hundred miles from the coast and there can be very few people who have not seen the sea.

Although the sea does not alter from place to place, the land next to it, which is called the coast, varies from rock walls called cliffs, to sandy beaches where we can sunbathe and swim.

These coastlines are changing all the time as the breaking waves pound on the shore. Many are also altered by the people who live in the area and build promenades, piers, harbours and so on.

Some of the beautiful stretches of our coast are now owned by organizations such as The National Trust. Organizations of this kind preserve the coastline and stop it being spoilt by development. At the same time anyone can walk in these areas whenever they wish and enjoy the scenery.

This book describes some of these coasts and explains how they are formed.

How cliffs are formed

Where high land slopes down steeply into the sea, the waves pound against it and cut, or erode, a horizontal notch into the rocks at the level of the surface of the water. As the notch is cut deeper and

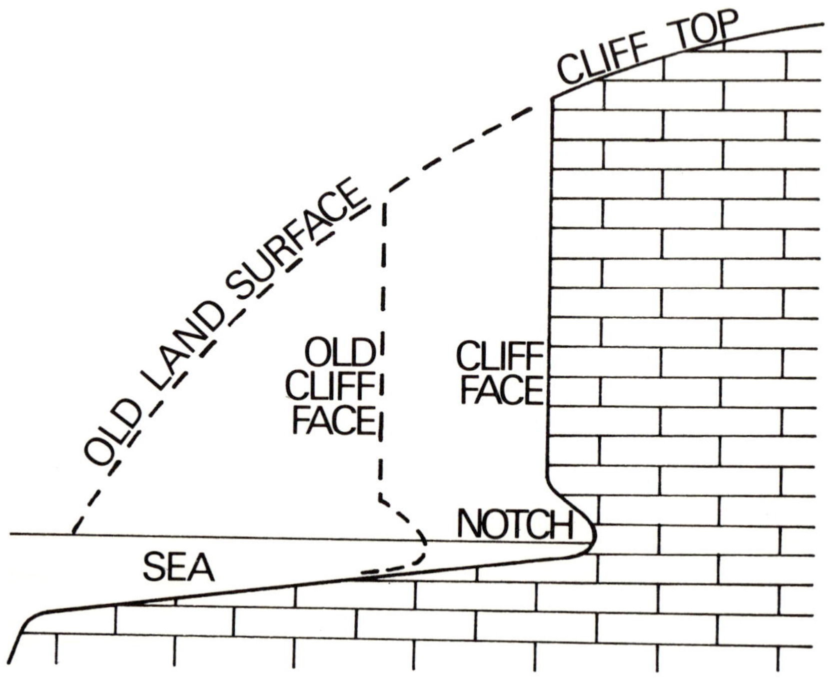

deeper into the land, the rocks above have nothing under them for support and they break away leaving a wall of rock called a cliff.

As the waves continue to cut into the land, rather like a giant saw at the base of the cliff, the rocks above the notch fall into the sea and the cliff face moves inland. At the same time it becomes higher and higher.

As the cliff is cut back by the action of the sea, a flat rock surface is left in front of it. This is called the wave cut platform. Pieces of rock which have fallen from the cliff face can be found scattered all along this stretch of shoreline. The waves attack these rocks and eventually break them into smaller pieces of rock, pebbles, shingle and sand.

At low tide some of the wave cut platform is above the sea level and small hollows in the rock become rock pools full of sea water. These pools often have small plants and creatures living in them such as anemone, limpets, barnacles, small crabs and seaweed.

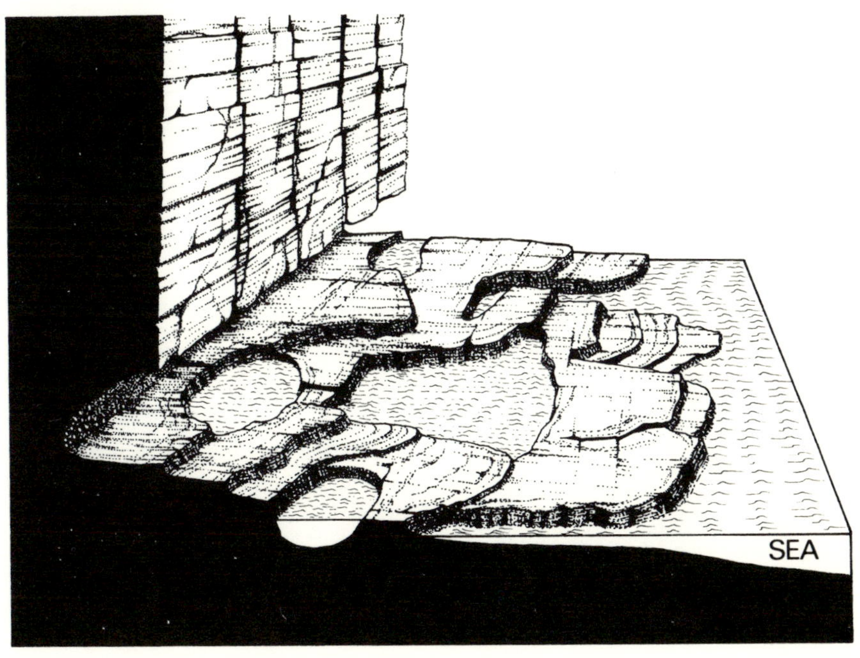

Not all cliff faces are alike. Their appearance depends upon the type of rock into which the waves cut. If the cliff is made up entirely of one type of rock, the shape of the cliff depends on how well the rock can resist the sea and rain water attacking it.

Where the waves erode rock that is not very resistant, such as shale, rain falling on the cliff will wash away the top of the cliff more rapidly than the waves can undercut the base. As a result the cliff face becomes curved or convex in shape.

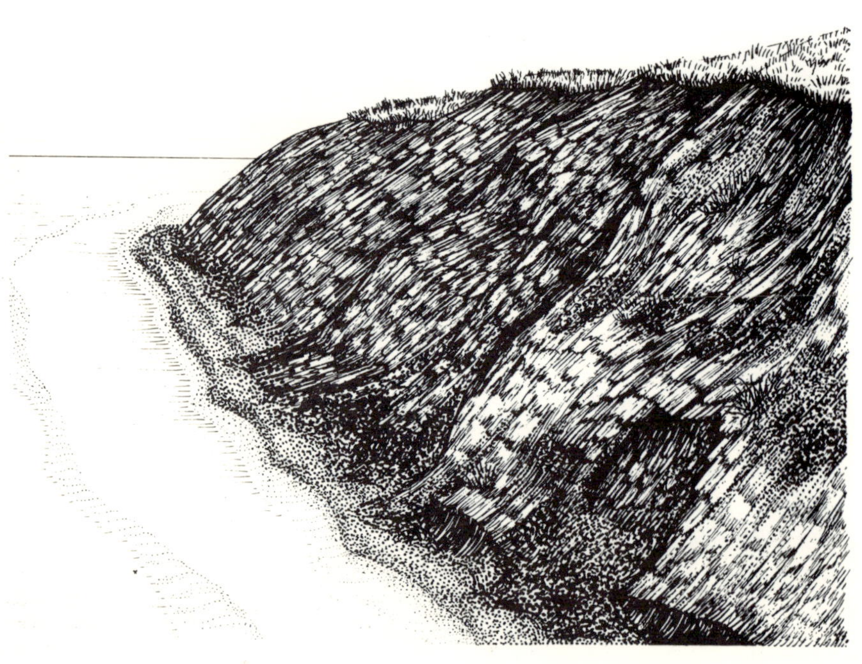

Where the cliff is made up of a resistant rock such as granite, or rock that is permeable and soaks up rain water, such as chalk or limestone, the base of the cliff is undercut much faster than the surface is washed away by the rain and the cliff face is always vertical.

Clay is a very soft rock — so soft that you can

break it up in your hand — but despite this it can form very steep cliffs. They occur where the sea cuts very quickly into an outcrop of clay that slopes steeply into the water. As the sea erodes the base of the slope, the clay above the notch falls constantly into the sea leaving the cliff with a steep face.

Where the sea is cutting slowly into the clay, the soft rock in the cliff face becomes soaked with rain water and slumps to the foot of the cliff. The wave cut platform is covered with a jumbled mass of blocks of clay. Many of these blocks still have clumps of grass growing on them — grass that once covered the top of the cliff. Sometimes parts of the clifftop path, fence and even buildings, slip down the cliff face on one of these blocks as the rock on which they were built breaks away from the rest of the cliff.

Many cliffs are cut into layers of rock called beds. No two beds are of equal resistance and the less resistant ones break away faster than the others. The result is that the cliff face becomes a series of ridges and grooves. Each ridge is caused by a bed of resistant rock outcropping in the cliff face. The grooves between the ridges are outcrops of the less resistant beds of rock.

Where the beds in the cliff are horizontal, the

ridges look like shelves running along the cliff face and form convenient nesting sites for birds. Some have small pockets of earth on their upper surfaces where clumps of rock plants such as thrift or sea-pinks grow.

Where the beds slope, or dip, inland, the resistant beds form steps in the cliff face. Each step is the thickness of a bed of rock and the cliff is called a step cliff.

If the beds dip towards the sea, the resistant bed of rock on the surface forms a sloping cliff that looks like a giant slide dipping into the sea. Once this surface bed is cut into by the action of the sea, large

12

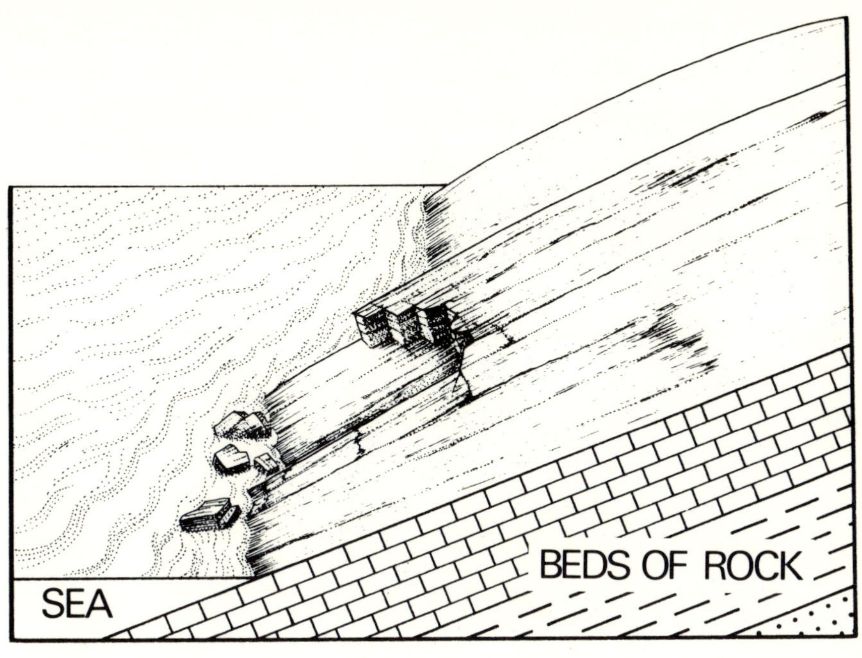

slabs of rock, the thickness of the surface bed, break
off and slide into the water and onto the wave cut
platform.   Eventually a lower bed of rock forms a
new sloping face to the cliff.

Caves and blow holes

Where there are cracks, called faults, in the cliff
face the waves cut into them faster than into the rest
of the cliff.   In this way the faults are widened and
become caves.

Some caves grow larger and larger as the waves pound into them and the walls crumble. Eventually, some caves grow so large that the roof — the rock between the ceiling of the cave and the cliff top — becomes very thin. As waves surge into the cave they trap air which, because it is compressed, blows a hole in the roof. This hole is called a blow hole.

On the cliff top you can look down into the cave below. In stormy weather jets of sea water shoot up through these holes and look rather like fountains on the cliff tops.

Arches, islands, stacks, needles and stumps

Where a wedge of land, called a headland, juts out into the sea, the waves erode it and cliffs are cut on both sides.

Often faults run through the headland and the sea widens them until they form caves. Caves at both ends of a fault will gradually be enlarged until the sea

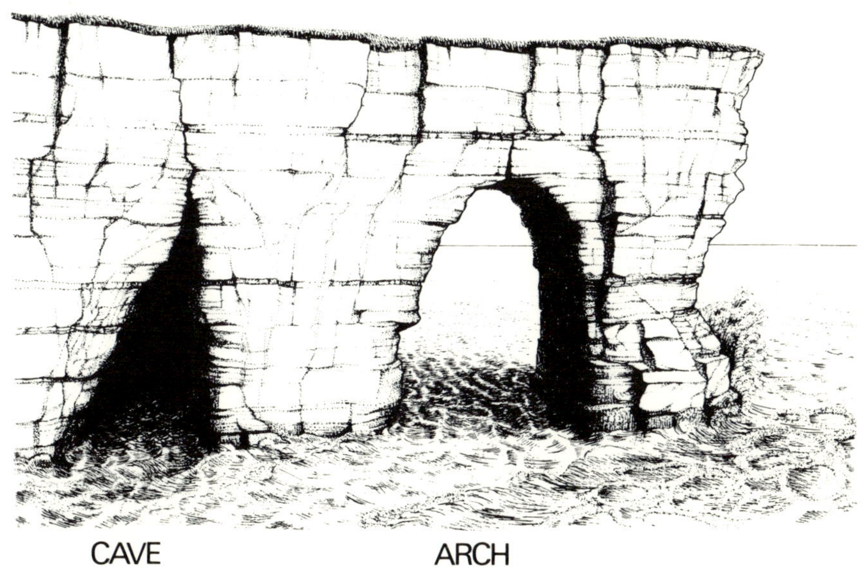

cuts through the back wall of one cave into the other. In this way the two caves become an arch.

As the sides and top of the arch are eroded, the top will eventually collapse, leaving part of the head-land as an island.

In turn the island is eroded and becomes smaller and smaller. An island that is no more than a pillar of rock with a flat surface is called a stack. When it is eroded still further and becomes a sharp point of rock, it is called a needle, and when the waves have cut away most of the rock that lies above the surface of the water, it is called a stump.

Many headlands, where they begin to jut out into the sea, have caves and then arches cut into them. They are then broken up into islands, followed by stacks, needles and lastly, stumps. Large stumps often make excellent sites for lighthouses.

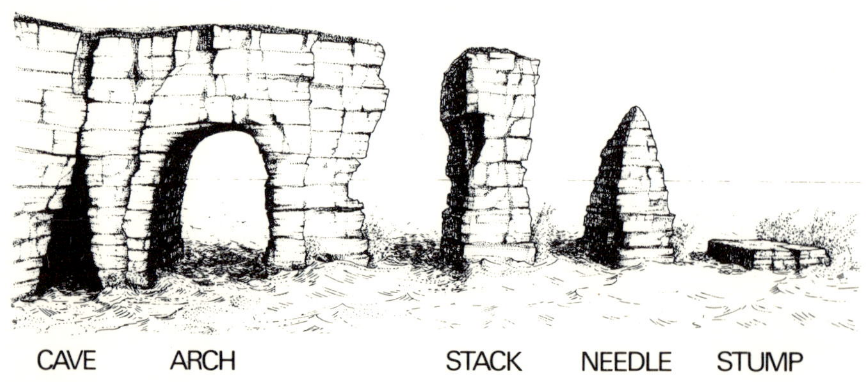

16

Rocks that fall from the cliffs are eventually broken up into large pieces which are rolled around by the sea and rounded until they form large pebbles. These in turn are worn down into smaller pebbles called shingle, even smaller pieces called grit and, at length sand.

This material is carried by the waves and is dropped on stretches of the coast that slope gently into the sea. As more and more material is dropped or deposited by the sea, it builds up to form a beach. The type of beach that forms depends on the type of material that the sea is carrying. Some areas

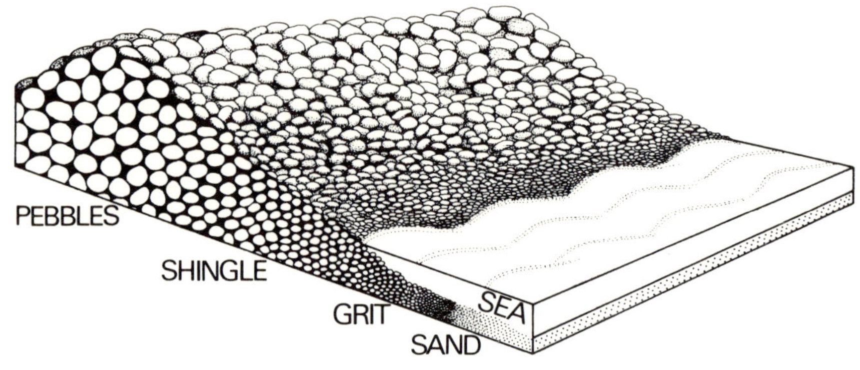

have pebble or shingle beaches, while others may be of grit or sand.

Where pebbles, shingle, grit and sand are all deposited in the same area, the waves throw all the material to the top of the beach. The water running back to the sea after each wave breaks — the undertow or backwash — washes back the finer material such as the sand. In the end the beach has large pebbles at the top, then a belt of shingle, then grit and lastly sand. Often the grit and sand stretches can only be seen at very low tide.

Storm beaches

A storm beach is formed on a beach that is made up entirely of pebbles or has a belt of large pebbles

18

at the top. When there is a storm the waves are very high and deposit a wall of pebbles across the top of the beach. This wall, called a storm beach, acts as a dam. As the waves break on the storm beach, the water pours over the top and ponds up behind the storm beach to form a lake called a lagoon.

After the storm, the lagoon drains very slowly as the water trickles through the storm beach and back to the sea.

Usually the local councils drive large pipes through the storm beaches to drain the water away before the lagoon has a chance to form and flood farmland and caravan sites.

Sand dunes

When a beach is made up entirely of sand, the sand at the top of the beach dries out and is blown inland by the wind.

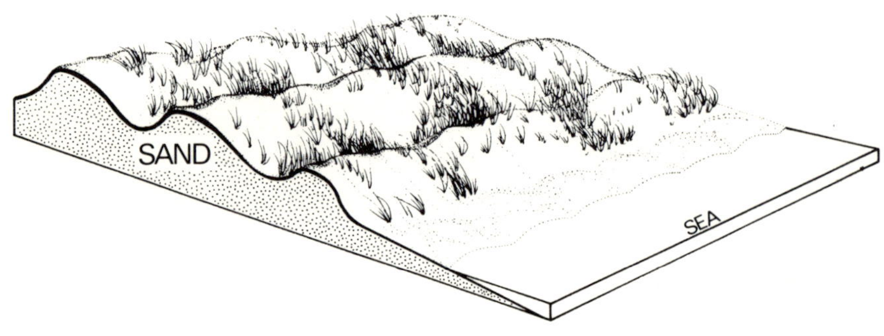

At the top of the beach the sand piles up against small bushes or clumps of grass. Once a mound forms more and more sand piles up on and around it until it becomes a hill of sand called a sand dune.

The wind blows the sand up the side of the dune facing the sea and drops it over the side of the dune facing the land. In this way the dune grows higher and at the same time moves inland.

Sand dunes can bury farmland, cover the base of trees and kill them and smother roads and buildings.

20

To prevent the dunes moving, people often plant certain types of fir trees and a special grass, called bent grass, that will grow well on sand.

Long shore drift

You have already seen how material is carried up the beach by the waves and how some of it is then carried back down the beach by the backwash. Waves very rarely break in a straight line along the beach. Usually they break at an angle to the beach and carry material along at this angle. Then the undertow rolls some of the material back down the slope of the beach.

Material moving up the beach at an angle and

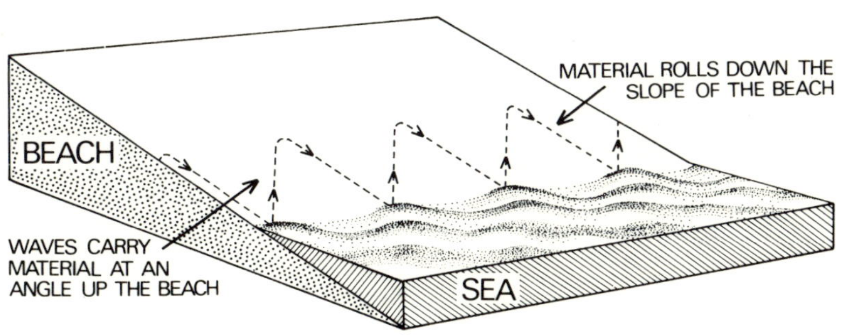

down along the slope, in this way, zig-zags along the beach. This zig-zag movement is called long shore drift.

Spits, bar and tombolos

Where a river flows into the sea, the mouth of the river forms a wide inlet of water called an estuary. When long shore drift is carrying material along the coast, it eventually reaches an estuary and the material falls into the water. More and more material

is deposited in the estuary and builds up into a ridge. This ridge of material, pushing out from one side of the estuary towards the far side, is called a spit. Material continues to move along the coast, then along the spit and, as it falls into the water at the end of the spit, makes it grow longer and longer.

Eventually a spit, growing out across an estuary, reaches a point where the river water has to push between it and the far bank of the estuary to reach the sea. At low tide the river carries out to sea any material deposited in its swiftly flowing water. At high tide the water surges inland through the gap and material is pushed behind the end of the spit to form a hook.

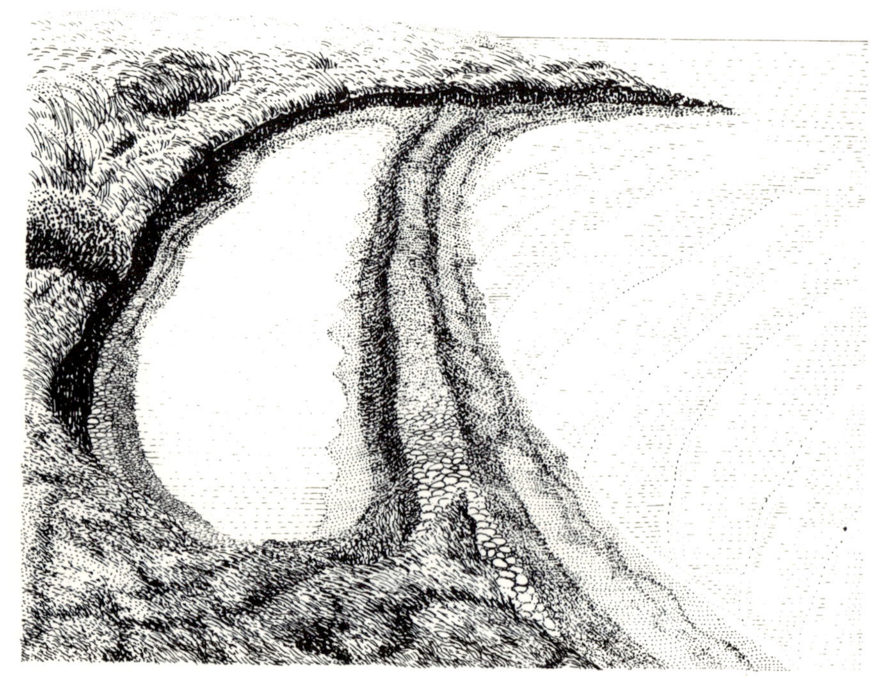

Where the river water is not flowing fast enough to push the material deposited out to sea, the spit continues to grow and reaches the far side of the estuary to form a bar. The water trapped between the bar and the coast is called a lagoon.

Sometimes the spit grows out and joins onto an island. It is then called a tombolo.

Very fine material, called silt, is carried by rivers to the coast. At the coast the silt is deposited in areas of calm salt water, for example, in the calm water behind a hooked spit, in the lagoon behind a bar and along the side of an estuary furthest away from the river current.

As more and more mud is deposited the level of the sea bed is built up. Eventually a stage is reached where the area is still covered by the sea at high tide

but, when the water recedes at low tide, it exposes flat stretches of mud called mud flats.

After a time, grass that will grow in salt water starts to grow on the mud flats and eventually covers the mud. Each time the tide covers the area it carries more silt and, as a result, more and more silt is trapped between the blades of grass growing on the mud flats.

Slowly the level of the mud flats are built up until the area is above the level of the water at high tide as well as low tide. The area has become a salt marsh.

Water drains from a salt marsh in a network of channels cut deep into the mud. At high tide the sea water fills these channels or creeks and people sail small boats into the salt marsh and anchor them, leaving them to settle on the mud at low tide.

Rias and fiords

Thousands of years ago the sea was at a much lower level than it is today and the weather was very much colder. In the south of the country rivers cut valleys as they flowed to the sea. In central and northern Britain it was too cold for the snow to melt and form rivers and, instead, it formed rivers of ice called glaciers. These glaciers also cut valleys as they moved to the coast.

The rivers cut valleys that sloped uphill on either side in a ' V ' shape, and wound or meandered to the sea. The glaciers cut straight valleys with upright sides and a flat floor.

The weather grew warmer and the ice melted. Water from the melting ice flowed into the sea which then rose to its present level drowning these valleys.

A drowned river valley is called a ria. The valley sides slope into the water and the deepest water winds up the centre of the ria following the path of the old river bed.

A drowned valley that has been cut by a glacier is called a fiord. It has very steep walls dropping into the water which is about the same depth from one side of the fiord to the other since the water has drowned a flat valley floor.

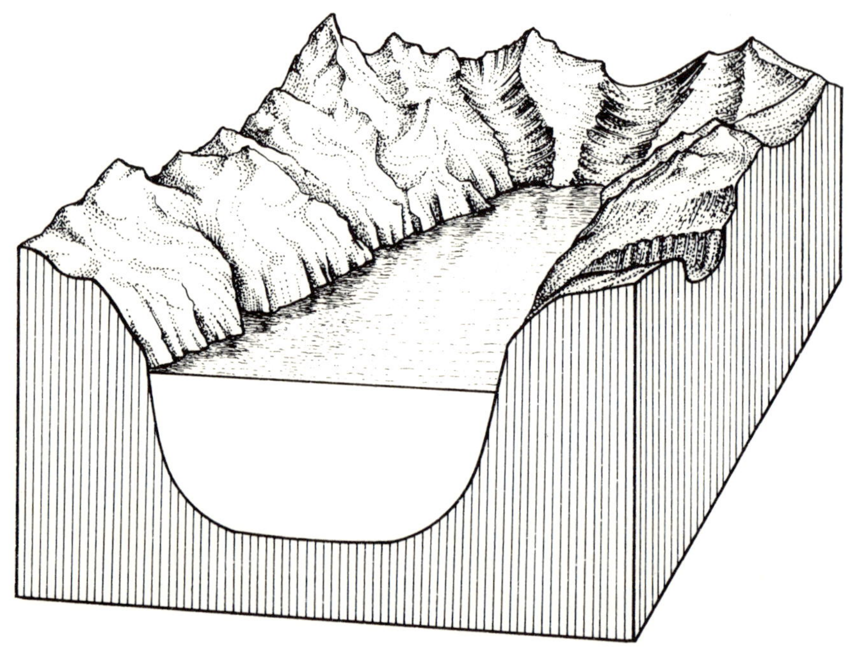

Both rias and fiords provide sheltered water for ships to anchor. Ships sailing up a ria have to be careful to sail along the line of deep water but it is easier to find sites for small ports on the gently sloping sides of the ria than on the steep cliffed sides of the fiord.

ENTERPRISE NEPTUNE

In 1965 The National Trust, having decided to increase its efforts to preserve as much of our beautiful coastline as possible, launched a scheme called "Enterprise Neptune". Work of this type is very important since, without it, much of the natural coastal beauty would be ruined forever by badly sited industry and haphazard building development.

The map on the next page shows some of the coastal areas which are now protected and controlled by The National Trust. If you would like to know more about the work of the Trust and Enterprise Neptune you should write to the address below.

Enterprise Neptune,
The National Trust,
42, Queen Anne's Gate,
London SW1H 9AS

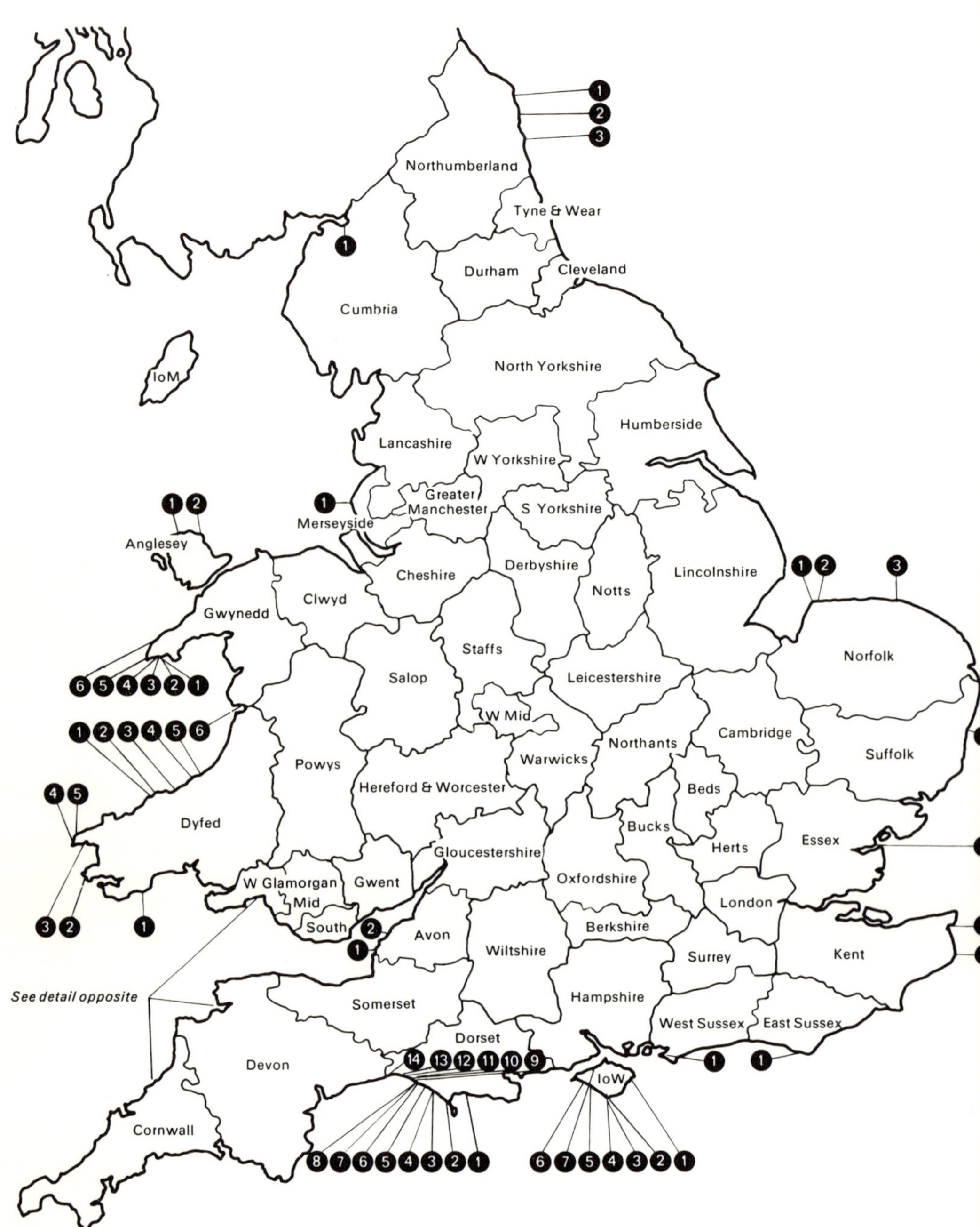

IoM
Northumberland
Tyne & Wear
Durham
Cleveland
Cumbria
North Yorkshire
Humberside
Lancashire
W Yorkshire
Greater Manchester
S Yorkshire
Merseyside
Anglesey
Cheshire
Derbyshire
Notts
Lincolnshire
Gwynedd
Clwyd
Staffs
Salop
Leicestershire
Norfolk
W Mid
Powys
Cambridge
Suffolk
Dyfed
Hereford & Worcester
Warwicks
Northants
Beds
Bucks
Essex
Gloucestershire
Herts
W Glamorgan
Gwent
Mid
Oxfordshire
London
South
Avon
Berkshire
Wiltshire
Kent
Surrey
See detail opposite
Somerset
Hampshire
West Sussex
East Sussex
Dorset
Devon
IoW
Cornwall

AVON

1 Middle Hope (Woodspring)
2 Redcliffe Bay

CORNWALL

1 Trethill Cliffs
2 Bodigga Cliff, Looe
3 Lansallos Barton
4 Polruan
5 Fowey
6 The Gribbin
7 Black Head, St Austell Bay
8 Lamledra
9 Penare
10 Penquarry, Hemmick
11 Hemmick Beach
12 Lambsowden Cove
13 Ardevora
14 Tregassick Farm
15 Trewince
16 Carwinion
17 Frenchman's Creek
18 Penarvon Cove
19 Treleaver Farm and Beagles Point
20 Inglewidden, Lizard
21 Bass Point
22 Predannack, The Lizard
23 Meres Cliff, Polurrian Cove
24 Poldhu Cove
25 Rinsey Cliff
26 Lesceave Cliff

27 Marazion
28 Rospletha Cliff, St Levan
29 St Levan Cliffs
30 Zennor Head
31 St Agnes Beacon
32 Holywell Bay
33 Beacon House
34 Pendarves Point
35 Park Head
36 Porthcothan
37 Camel Estuary
38 Pentireglaze Farm
39 Middle Hendra, Treharrock
40 Tregardock
41 Tregonnick Tail
42 Valency Valley
43 Rusey Cliff, Crackington
44 Crackington Haven
45 The Dizzard, Crackington
46 Houndapit Cliffs
47 Stowe Cliffs
48 Coombe
49 Tidna Shute, Morwenstow

CUMBRIA

1 Solway Commons

SOUTH DEVON

1 Weston Cliffs
2 Weston Combe and Weston Mouth

3   Higher Dunscombe Cliffs
4   Dunscombe
5   Little Dartmouth
6   Beesands Cliff
7   Prawle Point
8   Gammon Head
9   Moor Sand Cove
10 Venericks Cove
11 Southdown, Thurlestone
12 Yealm Estuary

NORTH DEVON

13 Welcombe and Marsland Mouths
14 Fatacott Cliffs
15 The Brownshams, Clovelly
16 Burrough Farm
17 Baggy, Croyde
18 Lundy
19 Morte Point
20 Damage Cliffs
21 Ulfred Point, Lee
22 Lanleigh Valley
23 Torrs Walks
24 Golden Cove
25 The Great Hangman, Combe Martin
26 Holdstone Down
27 North Cleave, Heddon's Mouth
28 Woody Bay
29 Countisbury Hill and The Foreland. Lynmouth

KENT

1   Pegwell Bay
2   The Leas, St Margaret's Bay

MERSEYSIDE

1   Formby Point

NORFOLK

1   Holme-next-the-sea
2   Brancaster
3   West Runton Cliffs

NORTHUMBERLAND

1   Newton Links
2   Howick
3   Alnmouth

SUFFOLK
1   Dunwich Heath

EAST SUSSEX
1   Birling Gap

WEST SUSSEX

1   East Head, West Wittering

WALES

GWYNEDD

Anglesey
1   Cemlyn Estate
2   Boston Estate

Caernarvon

1   Penrallt Neigwl
2   Tyn-y-parc
3   Mynydd Bach
4   Porth Ysgo
5   Pen-y-cil
6   Porth Colmon

DYFED

Cardigan

1   Clos-y-Graig
2   Llwynysgaw
3   Llanborth
4   Lochtyn
5   Caerllan Farm, Cwmtydi
6   Ynyshir, Eglwys — Fach

PEMBROKE

1   Manorbier Cliffs
2   Kete
3   St Elvis, Solva
4   St David's Bay
5   Trleidir

WEST GLAMORGAN

1   Nicholaston Burrows
2   Pilton Green and Pitton Cross
3   Worms Head, Rhosili Beach and Mewslade
4   Rhosili Down
5   Whitford Burrows
6   The Bulwark
7   Ryers Down
8   Llanrhidian Marsh
9   Welsh Moor

The Trust also preserves coastal areas in Northern Ireland.

Model of Sand Dunes (1 & 2)

Using a rectangle of light cardboard, fold it as shown in diagrams 1 and 2. Use your own measurements for 'X' depending on how large you want the sand dunes to be.

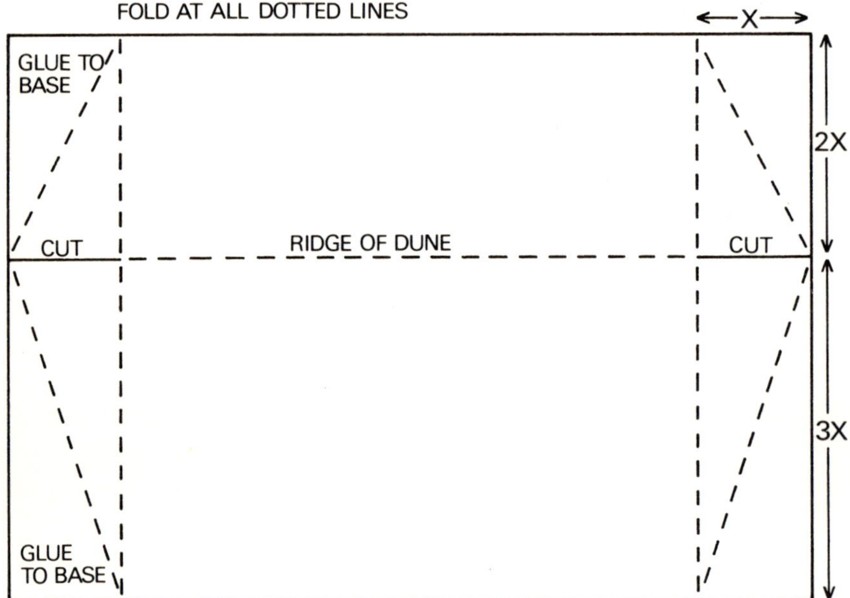

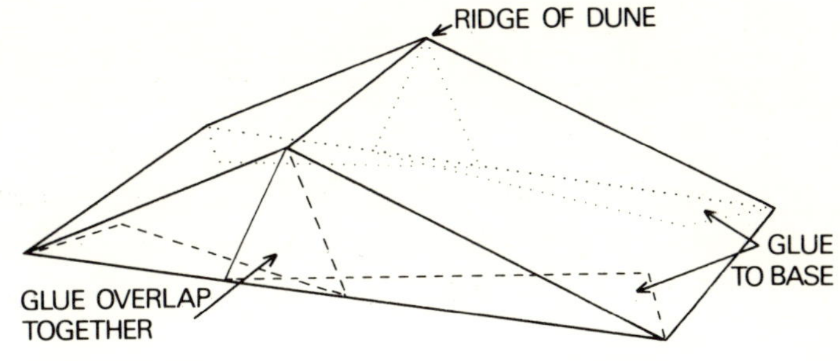

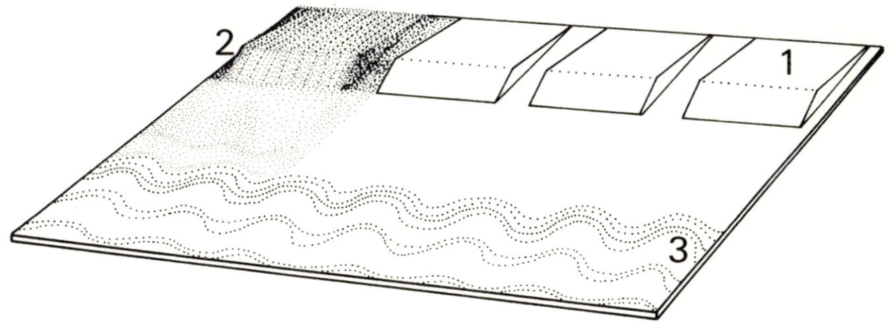

Position the model dunes as shown at 1 and cover them with thin fabric or paper (2) to make rounded edges. You can cover the beach and dunes with glue and then sprinkle sand all over to add realism. Show the waves of the sea at 3 and use white paint to indicate where the waves break.

Model of a Cave and Blow Hole

Prepare a base either from cardboard or from several
sheets of polystyrene as shown at H. Next, follow
the diagram at A and prepare the face of the cliff
from a long strip of cardboard which should then be
glued into position as at G. Small pieces of cardboard,
folded as shown (B), will help to stick the model
together.

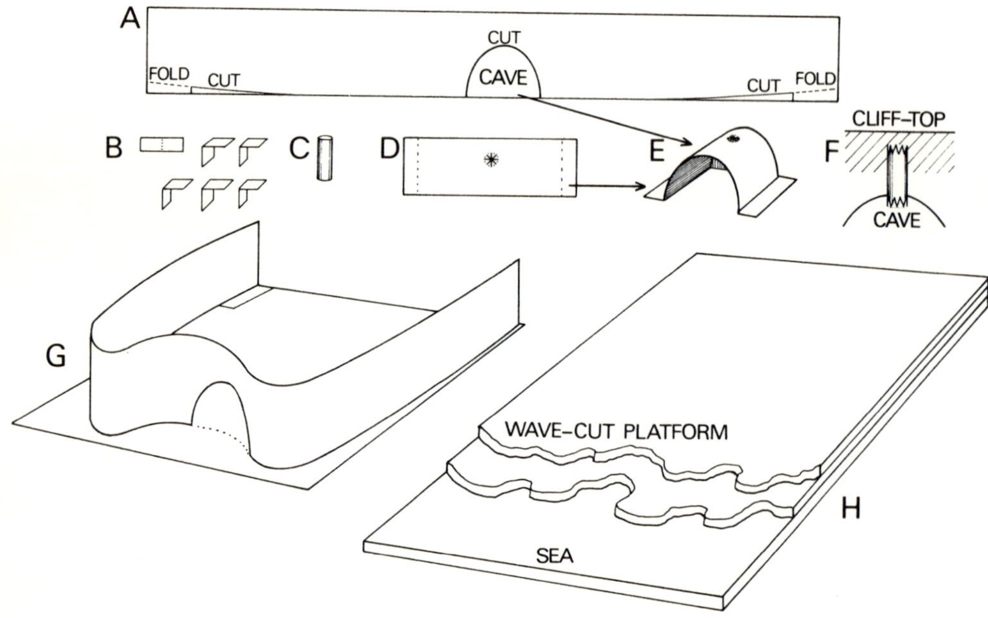

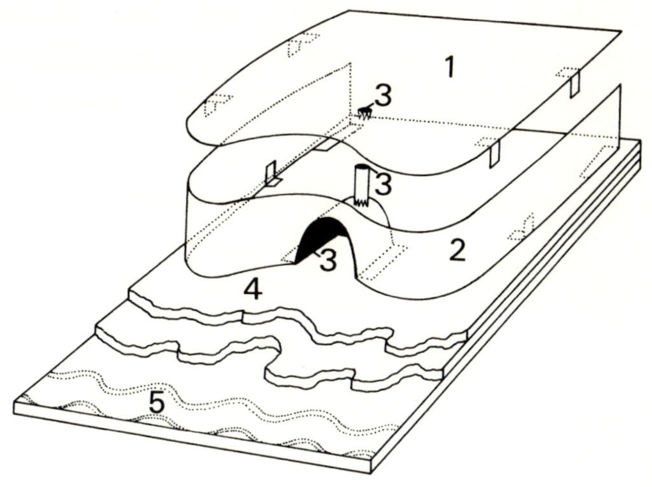

Insert the walls of the cave as shown at D and E taking care to position the cardboard tube, C, in the roof of the cave as shown at F. Now prepare the top of the cliff and affix it to the rest of the model as shown in the final diagram.

The numbers are suggestions for colours; 1 is green, 2 is grey, 3 is black, 4 is dark grey and 5 is blue. Try to mix other materials with the paints to make the textures more interesting.

Model of a Lighthouse

The diagrams show how to construct a model light-house which you can use with other models. Where paper is used for the roof and the support, you should glue side B under side A. Use a yellow marble for the light and cardboard or cotton reels for the tower

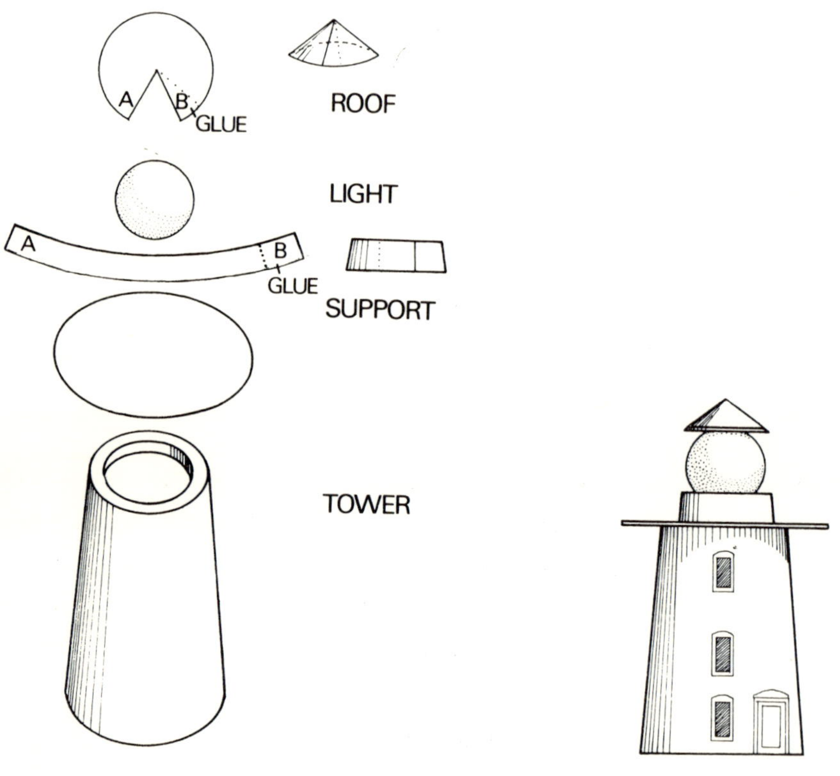

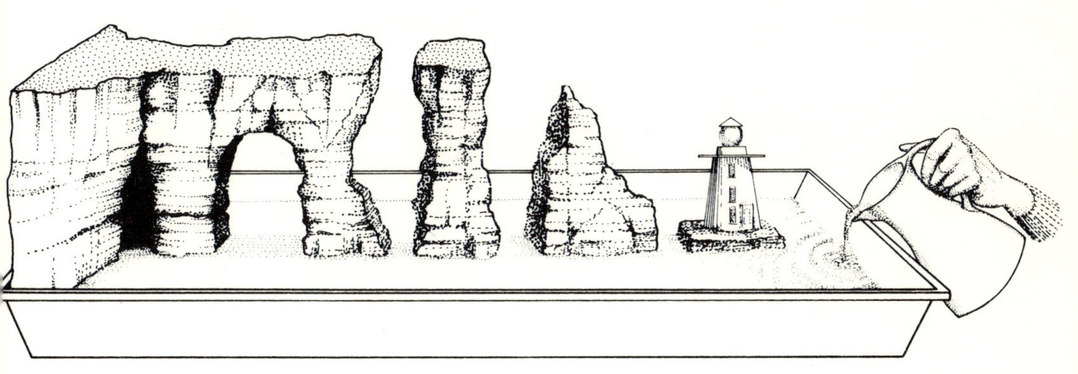

Using plasticine and a large metal or plastic tray try to reconstruct the features which have just been mentioned.

Model of a Rock Pool

Take a cardboard box and cut out the shape shown in diagram 1. Put some crumpled newspaper in the

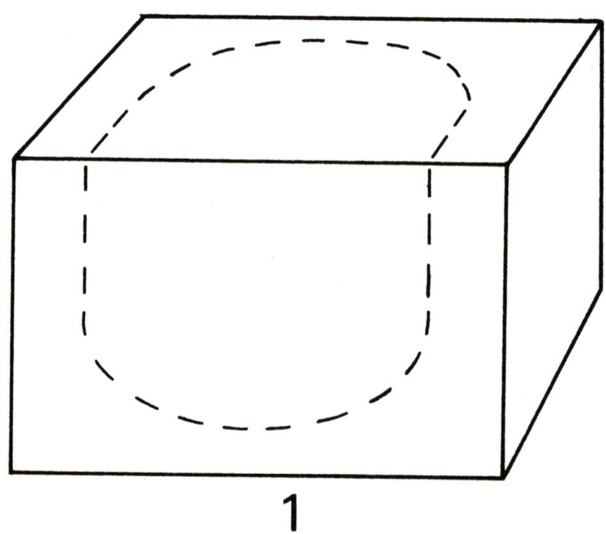

bottom of the box to support the base of the pool
(diagram 2). Take a large sheet of paper, which is

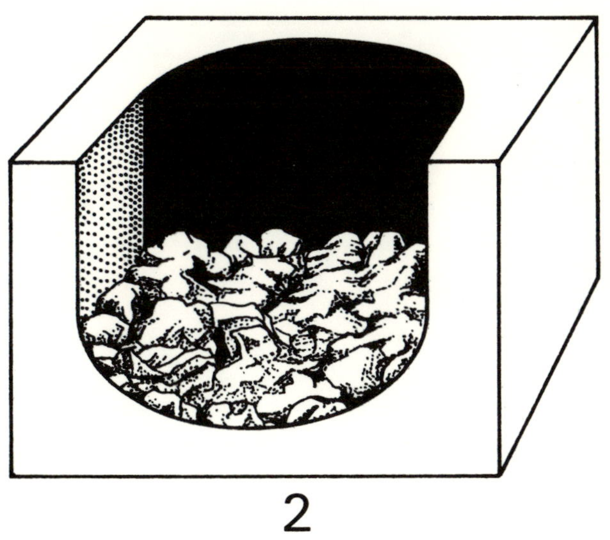

2

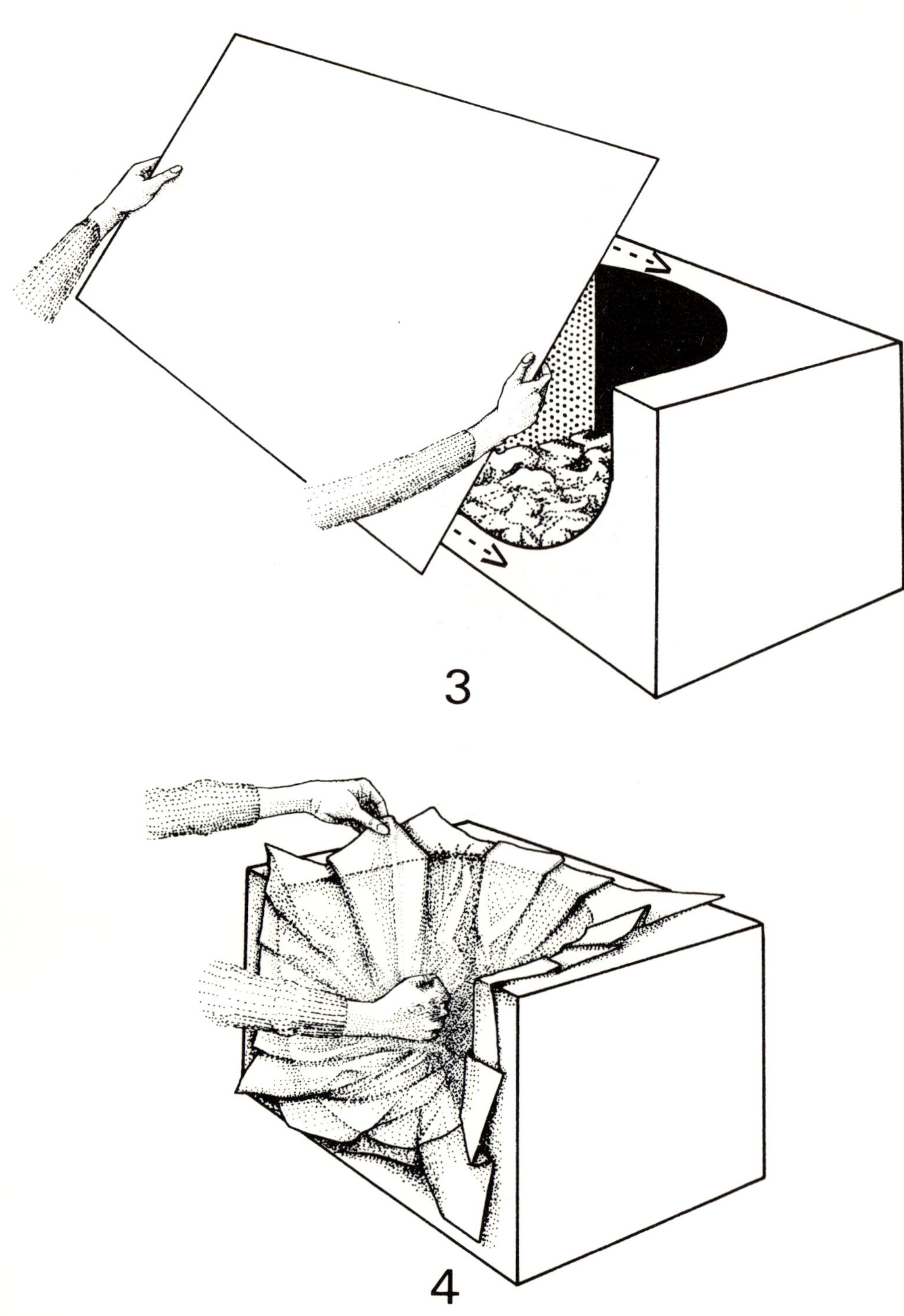

3
4

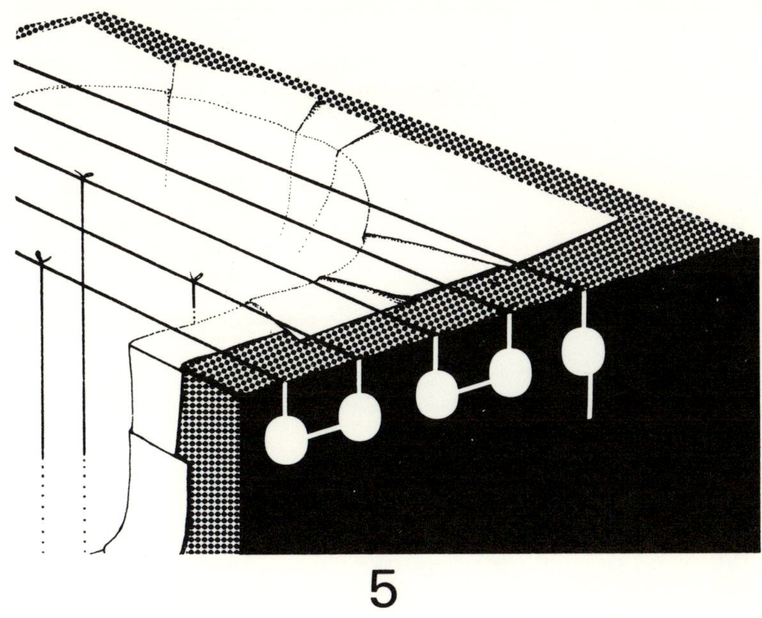

twice as long and twice as high as the box, and push it into shape as shown in diagrams 3 and 4 before sticking it into position. Fix drawing pins along both sides of the top of the box (see diagram 5) and wind thread from one side to the other. This is for suspending the various creatures.

Try to use as many real things as possible in your rock pool such as shells, sand and seaweed. However, if this is not possible, remember that you can model most things from paper, cardboard and plasticine. Small, brightly coloured fish can be made from silver paper and suspended from thread. Use the drawing of a rock pool to get ideas for models and the diagram to make different sized models of anemones.

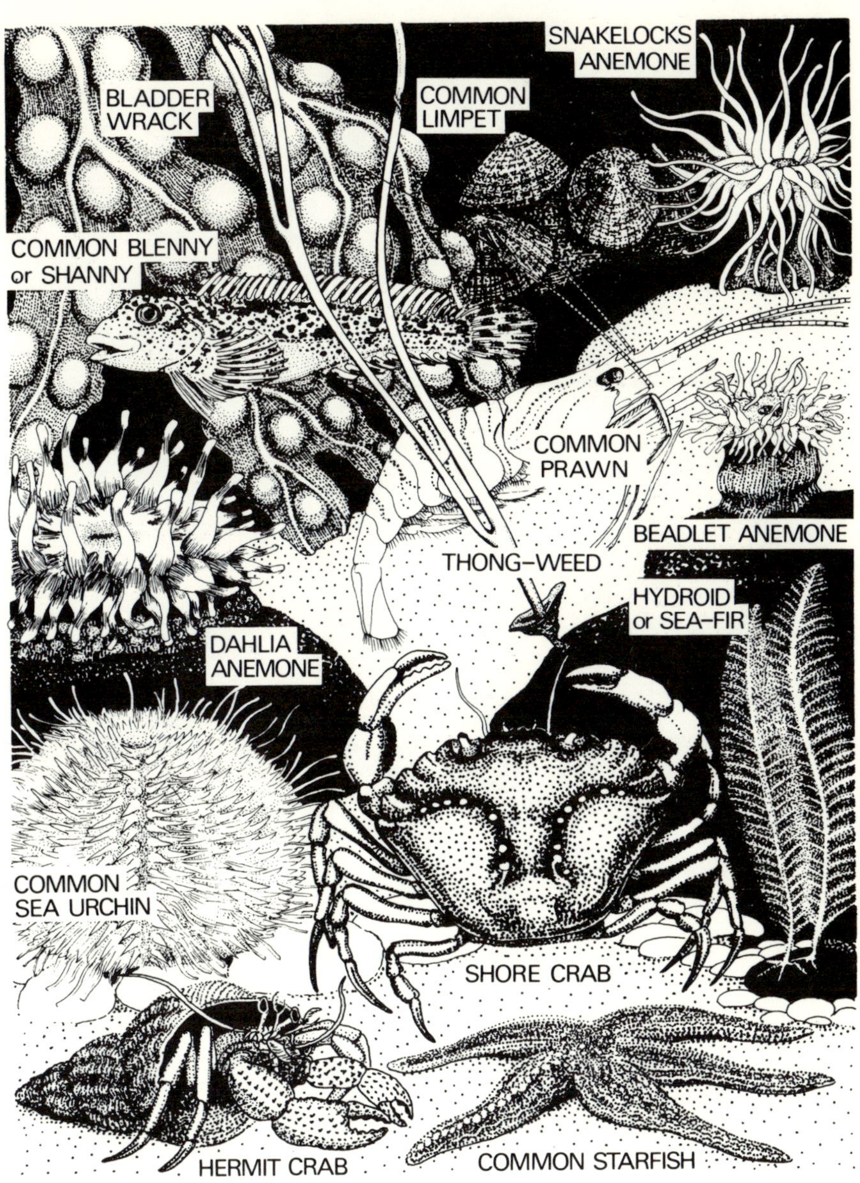

BLADDER WRACK
COMMON BLENNY or SHANNY
COMMON LIMPET
SNAKELOCKS ANEMONE
COMMON PRAWN
BEADLET ANEMONE
THONG-WEED
HYDROID or SEA-FIR
DAHLIA ANEMONE
COMMON SEA URCHIN
SHORE CRAB
HERMIT CRAB
COMMON STARFISH

Crossword A

Across

1 Dunes are made of piles of – – – – .

4 At the foot of the cliff is the wave cut
– – – – – – – – .

5 It has eight legs and lives in a pool

8 A spit that grows until it joins onto an
island.

9 Land jutting   out to sea is called a
– – – – – – – – .

11 Anemone live in a rock – – – – .

Down

1 See 10 down.

2 The waves cut a – – – – – – at the base of
the cliff.

3 Drains are laid through a – – – – – –
– – – – – – to drain the water from the
lagoon.

6 When the roof of a cave collapses a
– – – – – – – – – is formed.

7 A small pointed island is called a
– – – – – – – .

10 Sand moving along a beach is called
– – – – (1 down) – – – – – – drift.

Crossword B

Across

1   An island with steep sides and a flat top.

3   A cliff that looks like a stairs is called a — — — — cliff.

5   A drowned river valley.

7   Sea pinks are also called — — — — — — —.

8   It has two shells and lives in a rock pool.

10   A part of the coast where the sea curves into the land.

11   A hole cut through a headland is called an — — — —.

Down

2   A steep wall of rock is called a — — — — — —.

3   When long shore drift builds out a ridge of sand into the sea it is called a — — — — —.

4   The wide mouth of a river is called an — — — — — — — —.

6   An example of resistant rock is — — — — — — — —.

9   An example of soft rock is — — — — —.

Crossword C

Across

1   See 9 across

3   A large hole in a cliff is called a — — — — .

5   An example of permeable rock is — — — — — — — — — .

8   — — — — — — — is not as fine as grit.

9   — — — (1 across) — — — — — are covered by the sea at high tide but not at low tide.

10   A plant that grows in the sea.

Down

2   They cling onto the rocks in rock pools.

3   The land next to the sea is called the — — — — — .

4   They have tentacles and live in rock pools.

5   A salt water lake.

6   A mud flat, above the water at high tide, is called a — — — — marsh.

7   Thrift is also called sea — — — — — — .

THE COAST

Answers to Crosswords. A.

Across
1   Sand
4   Platform
5   Crab
8   Tombolo
9   Headland
11   Pool

Down
1   Shore
2   Notch
3   ·   Stormbeach
6   Blowhole
7   Needle
10   Long

Answers to Crossword B.

Across
1   Stack
3   Step
5   Ria
7   Thrift
8   Barnacle
10   Bay
11   Arch

Down
2   Cliff
3   Spit
4   Estuary
6   Granite
9   Clay

Answers to Crossword C.

Across
1   Flats
3   Cave
5   Limestone
8   Shingle
9   Mud
10   Seaweed

Down
2   Limpets
3   Coast
4   Anemone
5   Lagoon
6   Salt
7   Pinks